We Were There

We Were There

A Way of the Cross

Robert D. Eimer, O.M.l.
Sarah A. O'Malley, O.S.B.

**Illustrated
by
Mary Charles McGough, O.S.B.**

A Liturgical Press Book

THE LITURGICAL PRESS
Collegeville, Minnesota

To Sr. Mary Charles McGough, O.S.B.,
who has skillfully illustrated both
Journey of Decision and *We Were There.*
We are grateful to her for her
artistic talents which continually lift the spirit
and give glory to God.

We thank Rose Lee Eilering, Lisa Beck, and Barb Kaiser for typing the manuscript. Their patience is much appreciated. We likewise thank Sr. Lucille Geisinger, O.S.B., for proofreading the manuscript. We also thank Jo Ann Yeoman for her critique of the script.

Cover design by Ann Blattner.
Illustrations by Mary Charles McGough, O.S.B.

Excerpts are taken from the New American Bible, © 1991, 1986, 1970 by the Confraternity of Christian Doctrine, 3211 Fourth Street N.E., Washington, DC 20017-1194 and are used by permission of the copyright holder. All rights reserved.

ISBN 0-8146-2355-7

2   3   4   5   6   7   8

INTRODUCTION

The traditional Way of the Cross includes scenes that are based on pious traditions as well as scenes from the Gospels. For instance, the three falls of Jesus and Veronica wiping Jesus' face are not biblical scenes. In 1991 Pope John Paul II reshaped the Way of the Cross to include only those stations found in Scripture. We have taken his fourteen scriptural scenes and adapted them for *We Were There*.

John Paul II's Way of the Cross begins in the Garden of Gethsemane and concludes with the burial of Jesus. The various stations include characters who either reject or accept Jesus. Fr. Henri Nouwen has said that in encountering the cross, people have always been confronted with the choice of becoming either Christ's disciples or his executioners. Using John Paul II's scriptural stations, *We Were There* portrays scriptural characters that confront us like a mirror: do we accept Jesus or do we, by our sins, reject him? Are we followers of Jesus or do we help execute him? Through our sins, we all share some responsibility for the death of Jesus, the Lamb of God who has *taken on* and *taken away* the sins of the world.

We Were There is a Way of the Cross intended for both individual and group use. Although it differs from the traditional stations, this new Way of the Cross can easily be imagined by the individuals, or it can be created very simply in tableau form for parish Lenten devotions. A few comments might be helpful:

1. The spirit of *We Were There* is one of participation and emotional involvement through the imagination. The use of imagination is important, for the imagination stimulates emotions such as sadness, repentance, or admiration. The characters are meant to touch us, not just intellectually, but also emotionally. They provide a dramatic reflection on

5

the station. The Scripture texts are important in setting the scene and the mood of the monologues. Each station focuses on a character who was intimately involved with Christ's passion and who exhibited his/her own strengths and weaknesses. The characters challenge us to participate by examining our own strengths and weaknesses.

2. *We Were There* uses the following format:

a) The traditional refrain of "We Adore You, O Christ" announces the station.

b) A Scripture passage is read.

c) A character from the Scripture passage is named and then a dramatic monologue is rendered.

d) A short prayer is recited by the congregation to respond reflectively to what was revealed in the monologue.

e) A verse of "Were You There" is used after each station; however, other songs can be substituted.

There are many ways *We Were There* can be used for groups:

1. The first is the more traditional way. The priest/presider handles all the parts except the monologues. The latter are read by lectors. We suggest a variety of lector roles; these can be handled creatively and practically by each parish. No memorization is needed but separate podiums are recommended for the priest/presider and the lector(s). In this way, the Scripture sets the scene and a separate lector handles the monologue.

2. The second way is more dramatic. The priest/presider takes the parts other than the monologues. *Several people* form a tableau of the scene, and the main character comes alive and presents the monologue, preferably by heart, but otherwise reading the monologue with skill and feeling.

3. Other creative ways are also possible. For example, the scene can be set up near the sanctuary on a special platform, and the characters who are seated in the sanctuary simply walk over and take their turns close to the scene.

Creating the setting for the stations can be done simply or elaborately. The first station might simply portray Jesus kneeling and Peter sleeping. Peter then comes alive and gives his monologue. If done more elaborately, Peter, James, and John may be sleeping and Jesus kneeling.

Any props or special lighting need to be used tastefully. Simplicity helps: a chair for Pilate with his wife at his side; a dagger for Barabbas; a whip for the soldier in the scourging scene. Costuming can be realistic (dress of Jesus' day) or modern (Jesus in a white turtleneck; soldiers in army uniforms). If necessary the number of actors can be reduced by having the actors take several roles.

We Were There can give new life to the Way of the Cross devotion. It can be a challenge for youth groups (having them present the Way of the Cross for the parish); for people in retreat ministry or for schools.

OPENING PRAYER

PRESIDER: Let us pray . . . .

ALL: **Loving Jesus, along your way of the cross,/ you met hardened soldiers, condemning priests, and compassionate men and women. As we walk that same way of the cross,/ let us search our innermost hearts,/ for they are capable of hardness or compassion,/ fickleness or faithfulness. Jesus, may we confront the dark side of our hearts/ and, through your grace, decide to remain your faithful and compassionate followers. Amen.**

THE FIRST STATION
Jesus Prays in the Garden of Olives

PRESIDER: We adore you, O Christ, and we bless you.

ALL: **Because by your holy cross you have redeemed the world.**

Then they came to a place named Gethsemane, and he said to his disciples, "Sit here while I pray." He took with him Peter, James, and John, and began to be troubled and distressed. Then he said to them, "My soul is sorrowful even to death. Remain here and keep watch." He advanced a little and fell to the ground and prayed that if it were possible the hour might pass by him; he said, "Abba, Father, all things are possible to you. Take this cup away from me, but not what I will but what you will." (Mark 14:32-36)

PETER

It was a pitch black night, a night in which even the stars hid themselves. James, John, and I had accompanied Jesus many times. Once, on a mountain top, we saw Jesus bright as a torch, shining in glory. I could have stayed on that mountain forever, happy to build a shrine there but, no, Jesus set his face toward Jerusalem. James is always telling me that I'm so impetuous. I speak without thinking. Why didn't I listen to him? Yes, I opened my mouth when I felt my Master was in danger. Wouldn't you have done the same? At Philippi, I took him aside and told him not to go to Jerusalem because there he'd face hostile leaders. Then Jesus said something to me that was like a slap in the face. "Get behind me, Satan." Satan. I deserved that because I didn't understand that the cross was the way to new life—not just for Jesus but for all of us. But back to that Thursday night in the garden. I'm ashamed to say that we weren't much company for the Master that night. I heard the sighs and groans of Jesus as he prayed alone in the garden. He told us to keep awake but our eyelids were too heavy. Yes, the wine made us sleepy, but even more, our hearts felt burdened with sorrow. At our last supper together, I boasted that although everyone else would desert him, I would never fail him. But I did fail him, I did, I did.

PRESIDER: Let us pray . . . .

ALL: **Jesus, just as your disciples were insensitive to your anguish,/ we too, are sometimes uncaring about those who are suffering emotional and mental pain. Awaken within us compassion/ so that we may be more *present* to the sufferings of others,/ and do what we can to lessen their burdens. Amen.**

Were you there when he prayed, "Thy will be done"?
Were you there when he prayed, "Thy will be done"?
Oh! Sometimes it causes me to tremble, tremble, tremble!
Were you there when he prayed, "Thy will be done"?

THE SECOND STATION
Jesus Is Betrayed by Judas and Arrested

PRESIDER: We adore you, O Christ, and we bless you.

ALL: Because by your holy cross you have redeemed the world.

Then, while he was still speaking, Judas, one of the Twelve, arrived, accompanied by a crowd with swords and clubs who had come from the chief priests, the scribes, and the elders. He came and immediately went over to him and said, "Rabbi." And he kissed him. At this they laid hands on him and arrested him. (Mark 14:43, 45-46)

JUDAS

I know you all want to ask the question, "Judas, how could you have betrayed the Master with a kiss?" But you have to understand. The dream, the dream of a Messiah and a kingdom, was all but dead. How was Jesus going to unite our people against the Romans if he continued to create division, breaking the Sabbath and insulting our leaders? Jesus had become a hopeless idealist—turn the other cheek, indeed! How could any Jew dare to say, "Give to Caesar what belongs to Caesar"? No, no, the dream was dead. Jesus had no intention of conquering the Romans. Instead of collecting money to build an army, this dreamer gave it away to the poor. Yes, I took money from the common purse. I wanted my share—what's fair is fair. Wouldn't you agree? There wasn't going to be any rich kingdom. Oh, I saw his power, the power over demons and sickness and even death. When I turned him over to the soldiers that night in the garden, I thought I'd force him to use his power against the Romans. I was sure he'd escape like he did in Nazareth when he magically made his way through a mob determined to kill him. I can't say I ever hated the Master; I simply became disillusioned, bitterly disillusioned. I made a tragic blunder in betraying Jesus and I paid for it. I regret that kiss, but it's too late . . . too late. . . .

PRESIDER: Let us pray . . . .

ALL: **Jesus, even though we have been unfaithful to you,/ you have remained faithful to us. Keep us mindful of our own human frailty/ lest we betray your trust in us. Unlike Judas, who turned away from you,/ may we turn to you for mercy and forgiveness. Amen.**

Were you there when Jesus was betrayed?
Were you there when Jesus was betrayed?
Oh! Sometimes it causes me to tremble, tremble, tremble!
Were you there when Jesus was betrayed?

THE THIRD STATION
Jesus Is Condemned by the Sanhedrin

PRESIDER: We adore you, O Christ, and we bless you.

ALL: **Because by your holy cross you have redeemed the world.**

The chief priests and the entire Sanhedrin kept trying to obtain testimony against Jesus in order to put him to death, but they found none. The high priest rose before the assembly and questioned Jesus, saying, "Have you no answer? What are these men testifying against you?" But he was silent and answered nothing. Again the high priest asked him and said to him, "Are you the Messiah, the son of the Blessed One?" Then Jesus answered, "I am; and 'you will see the Son of Man seated at the right hand of the Power and coming with the clouds of heaven.'" . . . They all condemned him as deserving to die. (Mark 14:55, 60-61, 62, 64)

CAIAPHAS

Annas, my father-in-law, sent Jesus to me with clear instructions: "Caiaphas, you know what you must do. He is a dangerous man." That crafty old fox, Annas, had spies watching Jesus for months. Finally they gathered enough evidence to arrest him and to send him to me for a trial. What caught the attention of Annas and myself, of course, was his arrogance—the arrogance to drive the money-changers out of the temple; the arrogance to allow the people to shout "Son of David" when he entered Jerusalem. Then finally came the rumors that he claimed to be the Messiah. After questioning his disciple, Judas, we decided to arrest Jesus secretly at night, away from the crowds. If we didn't act soon this so-called Messiah could incite a revolution and bring the Roman army crashing down upon us. No, no, it is better, far better that one man die than the nation be destroyed. Then came the trial. The witnesses were confused and unconvincing. If there was ever a slim hope of convicting him, I had to confront him with the key question: "Are you the Messiah?" Had he said "no," he could have walked away. But the simple-minded Galilean openly stated, for all to hear, that he was the "Glorious Son of Man." He blasphemed! And for that, he signed his own death warrant. What else could I do? Had you been high priest, would you have done differently?

PRESIDER: Let us pray . . . .

ALL: **Jesus, you suffered injustice at the hands of the self-righteous. As your followers,/ strengthen us when we must accept unjust treatment from others. Give us the courage to engage in the struggle for justice in our world. Amen.**

Were you there when Jesus was condemned?
Were you there when Jesus was condemned?
Oh! Sometimes it causes me to tremble, tremble, tremble!
Were you there when Jesus was condemned?

THE FOURTH STATION
Jesus Is Denied by Peter

PRESIDER: We adore you, O Christ, and we bless you.

ALL: **Because by your holy cross you have redeemed the world.**

While Peter was below in the courtyard, one of the high priest's maids came along. Seeing Peter warming himself, she looked intently at him and said, "You too were with the Nazarene, Jesus." But he denied it saying, "I neither know nor understand what you are talking about." So he went out into the outer court. [Then the cock crowed.] A little later the bystanders said to Peter once more, "Surely you are one of them; for you too are a Galilean."

He began to curse and to swear, "I do not know this man about whom you are talking." And immediately a cock crowed a second time. Then Peter remembered the word that Jesus had said to him, . . . He broke down and wept. (Mark 14:66, 67, 68, 70-71, 72)

MAID SERVANT

I was in the courtyard that night, a maid working for the High Priest Caiaphas. The soldiers whisked a man in through the back door. I told the other servants this must be Jesus of Nazareth. Then I saw a man who was a follower of Jesus—I was sure of it! He huddled near the fire hypnotized by its flames. I approached him—"No shyness in your bones, missy," my mother used to say—and I straightway asked him, "Are you a follower of that Nazarene, Jesus?" I didn't mean to alarm him, but he became startled at my words like a horse encountering a snake. "I don't know him," he sputtered. So I walked over to my fellow workers and pointed Peter out. I said loudly, so he could hear me, "Do you remember this man being a part of Jesus' group?" He turned sharply to us and denied it again. Finally, old Tobias, sitting around the fire, smiled at him and said, "Surely you are one of them; you're a Galilean!" (The Galileans have that strange accent, you know.) The man stood up, cursing and swearing. He became so violent, we scattered. But I watched him from a distance. I saw a strange look come over his face when he heard old Ben Rooster crow. It was as though death had called for his soul. Then he turned away, and I saw his shoulders rise and fall. If he weren't a man, I'd swear he was crying.

PRESIDER: Let us pray . . . .

ALL: **Jesus, out of fear Peter denied you/ but in the end was moved to repentance. Do not abandon us when we deny you out of human respect,/ but bless us with tears of repentance for our sins. Amen.**

Were you there when Peter denied the Lord?
Were you there when Peter denied the Lord?
Oh! Sometimes it causes me to tremble, tremble, tremble!
Were you there when Peter denied the Lord?

THE FIFTH STATION
Jesus Is Judged by Pilate

PRESIDER: We adore you, O Christ, and we bless you.

ALL: **Because by your holy cross you have redeemed the world.**

Now on the occasion of the feast the governor was accustomed to release to the crowd one prisoner whom they wished . . . . "Which one do you want me to release to you, [Jesus] Barabbas or Jesus called Messiah?" While he was still seated on the bench, his wife sent him a message, "Have nothing to do with that righteous man. I suffered much in a dream today because of him."

When Pilate saw that he was not succeeding at all, but that a riot was breaking out instead, he took water and washed his hands in the sight of the crowd, saying, "I am innocent of this man's blood. Look to it yourselves." (Matt. 27:15, 17, 19, 24)

PILATE'S WIFE

Pilate doesn't like it when I dabble in his affairs. "Leave politics to me. You're my wife—give your orders to the servants in the kitchen." But this time I was compelled to speak out. I had dreams about Jesus—frightening dreams, warning dreams, dreams that seemed to come from the gods. So I sent a servant to Pilate to inform him of my dreams. He scoffed at me, saying I should watch the foods I was eating. Still I could tell that he had listened. On that fateful day, as I stood by Pilate's side, I saw Jesus there, awaiting my husband's judgment. He stood there, with the dignity of a king, despite the cruel crown of thorns. I observed my husband trying to free Jesus, trying to find a way to save him till he realized that sparing Jesus might mean a revolt by the Jews. One more Jewish complaint to Caesar could have meant my husband's career. I wept quietly as Pilate washed his hands. Somehow I knew that my husband and I would never be the same, that we would be haunted forever by the Nazarene's innocence, his nobility, his gentleness. I was at Pilate's side on that fateful day, the wife of the man who condemned him. I had haunting dreams that I felt came from God. Have you ever resisted the voice of God?

PRESIDER: Let us pray . . . .

ALL: **Jesus, like Pilate, we too can resist the voice of God that comes to us from so many sources,/ including other people, events, and even dreams. May human respect, fear of failure, or the clamor of the mob/ never overpower the quiet voice of our conscience. Amen.**

Were you there when she warned him of her dreams?
Were you there when she warned him of her dreams?
Oh! Sometimes it causes me to tremble, tremble, tremble!
Were you there when she warned him of her dreams?

19

THE SIXTH STATION
Jesus Is Crowned with Thorns and Scourged

PRESIDER: We adore you, O Christ, and we bless you.

ALL: Because by your holy cross you have redeemed the world.

So Pilate, wishing to satisfy the crowd, released Barabbas to them and, after he had Jesus scourged, handed him over to be crucified.

The soldiers led him away inside the palace, that is, the praetorium, and assembled the whole cohort. They clothed him in purple and, weaving a crown of thorns, placed it on him. They began to salute him with, "Hail, King of the Jews!" and kept striking his head with a reed and spitting upon him. They knelt before him in homage. And when they had mocked him, they stripped him of the purple cloak, dressed him in his own clothes . . . ." (Mark 15:15-20)

SOLDIER

I was there when the rabbi was handed over to us, to have our fun with him. I'm just an ordinary soldier, not one to get involved in politics. I know how to handle this whip and I do my duty. I'm not bragging when I say I can turn a person's back into ribbons, red ribbons.

When we heard the rumors that Jesus was pretending to be a king—well, we've got some clowns in our outfit who love a little horseplay. We found some branches with thorns and wove a crown and threw an old purple cloak over his bleeding shoulders. Then we had our sport with him, kneeling before him like he was a king and hitting him on the head with a stick. Everybody got into the spirit of the thing, whistling and hooting, shouting, "Hail, King of the Jews!" It was nothing personal, you understand. It's what we get paid for—making people miserable. Jesus wasn't a bad fellow really; in fact, he was braver than most, standing there and taking our best shots. He didn't beg for mercy, not once. Well, they took him, you know, and made him king of the hill, they did. The hill of Golgotha, that is. You get my drift.

PRESIDER: Let us pray . . . .

ALL: **Jesus, in silence you suffered the cruelty and mockery of the Roman soldiers. Out of deep love for us you endured so much. May we see your face in every human being we meet,/ especially in the most persecuted and abandoned. Amen.**

Were you there when they crowned his head with thorns?
Were you there when they crowned his head with thorns?
Oh! Sometimes it causes me to tremble, tremble, tremble!
Were you there when they crowned his head with thorns?

THE SEVENTH STATION
Jesus Is Laden with the Cross

PRESIDER: We adore you, O Christ, and we bless you.

ALL: **Because by your holy cross you have redeemed the world.**

Now on the occasion of the feast he used to release to them one prisoner whom they requested. A man called Barabbas was then in prison along with the rebels who had committed murder in a rebellion. The crowd came forward and began to ask him to do for them as he was accustomed. Pilate answered, "Do you want me to release to you the king of the Jews?" But the chief priests stirred up the crowd to have him release Barabbas for them instead. Pilate again said to them in reply, "Then what [do you want] me to do with [the man you call] the king of the Jews?" They shouted again, "Crucify him." So Pilate, wishing to satisfy the crowd, released Barabbas to them and, after he had Jesus scourged, handed him over to be crucified. (Mark 15:6-9, 11-13, 15)

BARABBAS

Call me Jesus Barabbas or whatever name you like. I was part of a rebellion against the Romans that failed miserably. My only success was to kill a few of them before they captured me. Jerusalem knew me—I was a hero in the eyes of many of my people. Now the Romans were going to make an example of me, a leader of zealots. It would be the slow torturous death of crucifixion in typical Roman style.

I was brought before a shouting crowd along with another prisoner: Jesus of Nazareth. Strange that we both had the same first name. Pilate was offering the crowd the choice of freeing Jesus the Nazarene or Jesus Barabbas. It was my lucky day. They shouted for my freedom and his death. Frankly, I didn't understand this Jesus of Nazareth. He had no passion, no hatred for the Romans. He acted like a docile sheep when they mocked him or spat in his face. This strange rabbi accepted the cross without a murmur, as if he was predestined to carry it. Well, I shouldn't complain. I became a free man, free to go underground again, awaiting the opportunity to drive the Romans from our land. Yes, I was there when Jesus of Nazareth took my place on the cross. How about you? Were you in the crowd that Friday?

PRESIDER: Let us pray . . . .

ALL: **Jesus, Barabbas was set free/ while you, the innocent one, were put to death for the sins of all. With grateful hearts, we pour out our thanks/ for the many gifts you have given us through the cross, especially forgiveness of sin. Amen.**

Were you there when he bore the wooden cross?
Were you there when he bore the wooden cross?
Oh! Sometimes it causes me to tremble, tremble, tremble!
Were you there when he bore the wooden cross?

THE EIGHTH STATION
Jesus Is Helped by Simon the Cyrenian

PRESIDER: We adore you, O Christ, and we bless you.
    ALL: **Because by your holy cross you have redeemed the world.**

They pressed into service a passer-by, Simon, a Cyrenian, who was coming in from the country, the father of Alexander and Rufus, to carry his cross. (Mark 15:21)

SIMON OF CYRENE

For years I had dreamed of making a pilgrimage to Jerusalem for a Passover celebration. I had saved my money to make the journey across the sea from North Africa. When I arrived in Jerusalem, my eyes feasted on the golden splendor of the temple. Then my wife and sons, Rufus and Alexander, went to the market to buy food while I became a pilgrim, walking the crowded streets. I stopped to observe a pitiful procession of a criminal carrying his cross. Suddenly, before I realized what was happening, a Roman centurion seized me by the arm and forced me to carry this criminal's cross. I was bitter and angry. Under my breath, I cursed my rotten luck—wrong place at the wrong time. "All this way from Cyrene for what? This humiliation! Why did this happen to me, Simon, a poor farmer?" Then I saw the face of the man I was helping. He nodded as if to thank me. I will never forget that look! Suddenly the cross grew lighter and my heart became lighter, too. Later, when my family and I were baptized as Christians, I had a golden memory: I had helped Jesus bear his cross. As it turned out, it wasn't bad luck; it was God's blessing in disguise. My life was changed on the day I lifted his cross. What about you? Were you in that crowd that day?

PRESIDER: Let us pray . . . .

ALL: **Jesus, on your lonely journey,/ you welcomed the help of Simon, a passerby. At first he shouldered your cross with anger/ but later accepted it willingly. In truth, we all feel resistance to bearing the cross. Give us courageous hearts to bear our own burdens/ and generous hearts to share the burdens of others. Amen.**

Were you there when Simon helped the Lord?
Were you there when Simon helped the Lord?
Oh! Sometimes it causes me to tremble, tremble, tremble!
Were you there when Simon helped the Lord?

THE NINTH STATION
Jesus Meets the Women of Jerusalem

PRESIDER: We adore you, O Christ, and we bless you.

ALL: **Because by your holy cross you have redeemed the world.**

A large crowd of people followed Jesus, including many women who mourned and lamented him. Jesus turned to them and said, "Daughters of Jerusalem, do not weep for me; weep instead for yourselves and for your children, for indeed, the days are coming when people will say, 'Blessed are the barren, the wombs that never bore and the breasts that never nursed.' At that time people will say to the mountains, 'Fall upon us!' and to the hills,

'Cover us!' for if these things are done when the wood is green what will happen when it is dry?" (Luke 23:27-31)

ANONYMOUS WOMAN

I would rather not give my name. Just look upon me as an ordinary Jewish housewife. Together with several other God-fearing women, I did what I could for condemned prisoners. To alleviate their pain on the cross, we were allowed by the soldiers to administer a mixture of drugs and wine. Little good it did the poor devils. Weeping for these prisoners was part of the ritual expected of us. Very few, if any, tears were shed besides our own. We rarely knew the prisoners as persons until we met Jesus. He was not like any prisoner we'd ever seen carry a cross. Our leaders had accused him of breaking the law and blaspheming. Others claimed that Jesus traveled about doing good wherever he went. Who am I to judge—an ordinary Jewish woman? It was only when he stumbled in front of us and turned his face towards us that I realized how savagely he had been treated. My tears became genuine. Suddenly Jesus spoke to us, spoke as if he knew us personally: "Don't weep for me; weep for yourselves and your children." I felt a chill run through my body. His words resounded like a prophecy. I didn't understand what he had done wrong but I believed he was someone special. Could he have been—please don't mention who said this—could he have been the Messiah? What about you? What do you believe about Jesus?

PRESIDER: Let us pray . . . .

ALL: **Jesus, you asked the women to weep for themselves and their children. Give us the tears of true sorrow for our personal sins/ and have mercy on the sins of our generation. Amen.**

Were you there when the women wept for him?
Were you there when the women wept for him?
Oh! Sometimes it causes me to tremble, tremble, tremble!
Were you there when the women wept for him?

27

THE TENTH STATION
Jesus Is Crucified

PRESIDER: We adore you, O Christ, and we bless you.

ALL: **Because by your holy cross you have redeemed the world.**

They brought him to the place of Golgotha (which is translated Place of the Skull). They gave him wine drugged with myrrh, but he did not take it. Then they crucified him and divided his garments by casting lots for them to see what each should take. (Mark 15:22-24)

SOLDIER UNDER THE CROSS

Do you like to gamble? To listen to the click of the dice as you shake them? The excitement of gambling races through my blood. That day, as part of our pay, we were given a seamless garment: the robe of the Nazarene. The soldier with me raised his sword to divide the robe, but I stopped him. "Wait. Aren't you a gambler? Let's throw dice to see who gets the whole garment. Why spoil a good piece of cloth?" And you know what? I won the prize. As I held up the robe in triumph, I looked at Jesus. I heard him say, "My God, my God, why have you forsaken me?" Jesus wasn't concerned about losing his garment—no, he called out for his God; it was his God that he was clinging to. I watched him as he was dying and I could have sworn he nodded toward me, as if to say, "I'm glad you didn't destroy my robe. My mother made it." Probably all in my imagination, of course. Yet, I couldn't think of wearing that robe or even selling it. Instead, I gave it back to his mother. It was one of the few remembrances she had of him. I've always been a lucky guy. I was lucky to meet Jesus, even under the cross; lucky to win his garment and then to meet his mother. Did you see me that day, casting lots under the cross?

PRESIDER: Let us pray . . . .

ALL: **Jesus, the three hours you spent on the cross were hours of letting go:/ your robe to some soldier, your mother to John, and your life for the world. Teach us the difficult art of letting go,/ of dying daily to self/ so that at our last hour we may surrender our lives into your loving hands. Amen.**

Were you there when they crucified the Lord?
Were you there when they crucified the Lord?
Oh! Sometimes it causes me to tremble, tremble, tremble!
Were you there when they crucified the Lord?

THE ELEVENTH STATION
Jesus Promises His Kingdom to the Good Thief

PRESIDER: We adore you, O Christ, and we bless you.

ALL: **Because by your holy cross you have redeemed the world.**

Now one of the criminals hanging there reviled Jesus, saying, "Are you not the Messiah? Save yourself and us." The other, however, rebuking him, said in reply, "Have you no fear of God, for you are subject to the same condemnation? And indeed, we have been condemned justly, for the sentence we received corresponds to our crimes, but this man has done nothing criminal." Then he said, "Jesus, remember me when you come into your kingdom."

He replied to him, "Amen, I say to you, today you will be with me in Paradise." (Luke 23:39-43)

DISMAS

I was not so fortunate as my prison comrade, Barabbas. No crowd shouted for the release of Dismas. Since my cross was close to that of Jesus of Nazareth, I had a good chance to observe him. The rumor in prison was that Jesus was no thief or murderer; rather, he was innocent of any crime. Someone even mentioned he claimed to be the Messiah. That's why the other prisoners shouted at him: "If you really are the Messiah, do something. Use your power to free us." I told them to keep quiet. I was captivated by Jesus, by his gentle manner, his forgiveness of those who mocked him, but especially by the way he talked to God. He prayed like he knew God and was close to him like a son speaking to his father. Something about Jesus made me examine my life and see it for what it was: a life of deceit, thievery, and murder.

Once, when we were hiding in the mountains, a comrade told me about this Jesus and his message of forgiveness: how he ate with public sinners and risked offending the Pharisees; how he promised sinners a mysterious Kingdom if they only sought forgiveness. As I looked at Jesus with arms outstretched on the cross, I felt a deep peace and I was impelled to say, "Jesus, remember me when you come into your kingdom." I saw Jesus turn his head and say, "Today you will be with me in paradise." I was there and I became a believer. Have you become a believer, too?

PRESIDER: Let us pray . . . .

ALL: **Jesus, by offering salvation to the thief who repented,/ you gave hope to all sinners. Make us aware that your cross is a sign of forgiveness,/ even for hardened sinners. Lead us to accept your forgiveness so that, like Dismas,/ we too might be welcomed into paradise. Amen.**

Were you there when he promised Paradise?
Were you there when he promised Paradise?
Oh! Sometimes it causes me to tremble, tremble, tremble!
Were you there when he promised Paradise?

THE TWELFTH STATION
Jesus Speaks to His Mother and the Disciple

PRESIDER: We adore you, O Christ, and we bless you.

ALL: **Because by your holy cross you have redeemed the world.**

Standing by the cross of Jesus were his mother and his mother's sister, Mary the wife of Clopas, and Mary of Magdala. When Jesus saw his mother and the disciple there whom he loved, he said to his mother, "Woman, behold, your son." Then he said to the disciple, "Behold, your mother." And from that hour the disciple took her into his home. (John 19:25-27)

MARY

They called my son a criminal. How could that be? He healed the sick, fed the poor, preached a message of love; yet they called him dangerous and they nailed him to a cross. As I watched the soldiers raise him up on a cross, I wondered if they could understand a mother's heart. Can an executioner understand the miracle of a mother carrying a child in her womb for nine months? When Jesus was only an infant in my arms, Herod's soldiers tried to kill him, forcing Joseph and me to flee to Egypt. So many memories as I look back. Joseph teaching Jesus the carpenter trade; our panic when our son, a mere twelve year-old, was lost in Jerusalem; Joseph's peaceful death as he lay in my arms with Jesus at his side. I recall well the day Jesus put away the carpenter's tools to begin his Father's business. Those words, "his Father's business," have echoed in my heart since the time we found Jesus in the temple amid the teachers. Little did I know that his Father's business would lead him to Golgotha. I wonder if even he knew where he was headed.

When I saw my son dying, fading like a flickering candle, all that kept me going was faith, a faith in a loving, compassionate God. Before Jesus died, he made sure that I was taken care of. He gave the disciple John the charge of taking me into his home. In a way, John was already like a second son to me. The thought of losing my only son was overwhelming. But as I stood there with my sister and Mary Magdalene and the beloved disciple, I felt hopeful even amidst the biting pain.

I was there near the cross on that dark Friday afternoon. Were you there also?

PRESIDER: Let us pray . . . .

ALL: **Jesus, the mystery of suffering must have pierced the heart of Mary/ as she stood beneath your cross. At that hour, in the midst of her suffering,/ Mary became the mother of us all. May we find shelter beneath her mantle of care. Amen.**

Were you there when he said, "Behold your son"?
Were you there when he said, "Behold your son"?
Oh! Sometimes it causes me to tremble, tremble, tremble!
Were you there when he said, "Behold your son"?

THE THIRTEENTH STATION
Jesus Dies on the Cross

PRESIDER: We adore you, O Christ, and we bless you.

ALL: **Because by your holy cross you have redeemed the world.**

At noon darkness came over the whole land until three in the afternoon. And at three o'clock Jesus cried out in a loud voice, "Eloi, Eloi, lema sabachthani?" which is translated, "My God, my God, why have you forsaken me?" Some of the bystanders who heard it said, "Look, he is calling Elijah." One of them ran, soaked a sponge with wine, put it on a reed, and gave it to him to drink, saying, "Wait, let us see if Elijah comes to take him down." Jesus gave a loud cry and breathed his last. When the centurion who stood facing him saw how he breathed his last he said, "Truly this man was the Son of God!" (Mark 15:33-37, 39)

ROMAN CENTURION

I was there, a Roman centurion, part of the most disciplined war machine in the world. I was witness to all the events leading to his death. Even now my guilt haunts me when I remember what we did to Jesus in the courtyard: how we blindfolded him, and played vicious games, striking and spitting in his face. I watched the King of the Jews as he took up his cross. It was my official role to make sure he died that Friday. He was just another prisoner, another criminal to be crucified with Roman efficiency. But then I began to study this man—no, he was more than a man. It was his royal, noble manner, his undaunted courage. I had seen hundreds of men face death on the cross; they cursed and screamed. Jesus was different: he had a strange peace about him that went beyond anything I've ever seen. He even forgave the people under the cross who taunted him. In the end, Jesus died like a god, with dignity. Under the cross, I was driven to my knees, driven to recognize him for what he claimed to be: the Son of God. Within my heart, I felt the first stirring of faith and I asked Jesus to forgive my cruelty and hardness. I was there when Jesus died on the cross. Were you there? Did you recognize him, too?

PRESIDER: Let us pray . . . .

ALL: **Jesus, through your divine patience, goodness and forgiveness,/ you opened the eyes of the centurion. Deepen our faith/ so that we also might see you present in the patience, goodness and forgiveness of others. Amen.**

Were you there when he died upon the cross?
Were you there when he died upon the cross?
Oh! Sometimes it causes me to tremble, tremble, tremble!
Were you there when he died upon the cross?

THE FOURTEENTH STATION
Jesus Is Laid in the Tomb

PRESIDER: We adore you, O Christ, and we bless you.
ALL: **Because by your holy cross you have redeemed the world.**

When it was already evening, since it was the day of preparation, the day before the sabbath, Joseph of Arimathea, a distinguished member of the council, who was himself awaiting the kingdom of God, came and courageously went to Pilate and asked for the body of Jesus. Pilate was amazed that he was already dead. He summoned the centurion and asked him if Jesus had already died. And when he learned of it from the centurion, he gave the body to Joseph. Having bought a linen cloth, he took him down, wrapped him in the linen cloth and laid him in a tomb that had been hewn out of the rock. Then he rolled a stone against the entrance to the tomb. (Mark 15:42-46)

JOSEPH OF ARIMATHEA

My name is Joseph. I come from a town called Arimathea. I saw the drama unfold to the bitter end. I was with the council that planned his death, and although I did not support the council's action, I wonder if I did enough. Could I have stopped them if I had been more learned or more eloquent or more impassioned in my address to them? Was I perhaps afraid of the council, afraid they might discover that I was a secret disciple? Nicodemus and I were both hidden disciples, both afraid to follow him openly. But after his death, I cared little what the council would think. Jesus warned me about the use of riches for I am indeed a rich man. I was overjoyed when he accepted me as a disciple and allowed me to use my resources to support him. That was a privilege but not the greatest. The real privilege came when I asked Pilate for Jesus' body and buried him in a tomb meant for me. In the end, instead of burying Jesus in a pauper's grave, I had the consolation of serving him in death and unknowingly fulfilling the prophesy of Isaiah which said: "His tomb will be with the rich." I stood by when they closed the tomb. I was there on the day Jesus died for everyone, rich and poor alike. What about you? Were you there on that somber Friday?

PRESIDER: Let us pray . . . .

ALL: **Jesus, you gave Joseph the strength to break through the fears that bound him. Send upon us the power of your Spirit/ so that we may overcome all fear/ and announce the good news of your death and resurrection. Amen.**

Were you there when they laid him in the tomb?
Were you there when they laid him in the tomb?
Oh! Sometimes it causes me to tremble, tremble, tremble!
Were you there when they laid him in the tomb?

CLOSING PRAYER

PRESIDER: Let us pray . . . .

ALL: Jesus, we have journeyed with the characters of your passion/ and have seen the strengths and weaknesses within the human heart. We have discovered within us that same human heart,/ with its light and its shadows. Give us true humility to acknowledge our strengths and our weaknesses/ and to have a compassionate heart for others. Amen.

Were you there when he rose and conquered death?
Were you there when he rose and conquered death?
Oh! Sometimes it causes me to tremble, tremble, tremble!
Were you there when he rose and conquered death?